Ancient Egypt

Other books in the Daily Life series:

DAILY LIFE

Ancient Egypt

Don Nardo

KIDHAVEN PRESS

THOMSON
————— ✦ —————
TM
GALE

Detroit • New York • San Diego • San Francisco
Boston • New Haven, Conn. • Waterville, Maine
London • Munich

Library of Congress Cataloging-in-Publication Data

Nardo, Don, 1947–
  Ancient Egypt / by Don Nardo.
    p. cm. — (Daily life)
Includes bibliographical references.
Summary: Examines the daily lives of the people of ancient
Egypt, both rich and poor, including their sports,
recreation, religion, and view of the afterlife.
    ISBN 0-7377-0955-3 (hardback : alk. paper)
  1. Egypt—Social life and customs—To 332 B.C.—Juvenile
literature. [1. Egypt—Social life and customs—To 332 B.C.]
I. Title. II. Series.
  DT61 .N327 2002b
  932' .01—dc21

2001004962

Copyright 2002 by KidHaven Press,
an imprint of The Gale Group
10911 Technology Place, San Diego, CA 92127

Printed in the U.S.A.

Contents

CHAPTER ONE

Lives of the Wealthy and Privileged

Like nearly all societies in all ages, that of ancient Egypt had both rich and poor people. Most of the country's wealth rested in the hands of a handful of privileged individuals. A few thousand royal and noble families enjoyed lives of lavish comfort and leisure, while several million peasants and craftsmen lived much more simply and sometimes barely made ends meet.

At the top of the social ladder were Egypt's kings, known as **pharaohs**. Their word was law. And they dwelled in magnificent palaces, where people bowed deeply to them and hundreds of servants waited on them hand and foot. These rulers erected giant statues of themselves. Some of them also built the famous pyramids, massive stone structures used as tombs for themselves and sometimes for their wives and children. The largest of these structures still stand at Giza, near Egypt's modern capital, Cairo. The pyramids remain the most impressive evidence of the lofty power and status of the early Egyptian pharaohs. These men could marshal the

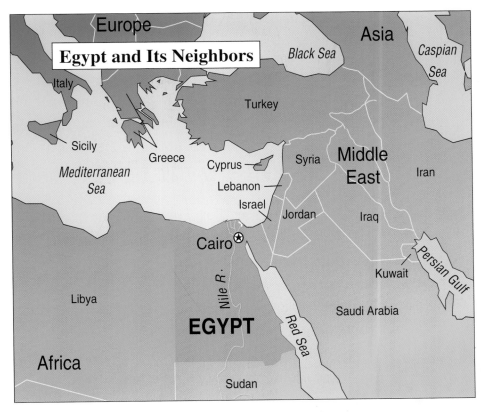

human and other resources of an entire country in order to help a single person reach the afterlife.

The high status of the pharaohs was not just a matter of their wealth and power. People saw these rulers as living gods. Each pharaoh was believed to be a child of Ra, the god of the sun, and therefore both different and better than other mortals.

Though the Egyptian nobles did not possess such godly status, they did enjoy great wealth and privilege. Among the nobles were the officials who administered the palace and the country's various districts for the pharaoh. Other nobles included the priests who ran the country's temples and a few rich landowners. Like the king, they and their families lived in large, comfortable homes and had many servants.

Upper-Class Homes

Most of what is known about the homes of ancient Egypt's royalty and nobility comes from two sources. The first consists of wall paintings found in the tombs of wealthy people. Also, the remains of the residences of a few of the pharaohs have survived. Studies of these artifacts show that each palace, temple residence, and wealthy home was like a little world unto itself. Each lay in the center of a large estate. Part or all of the grounds were surrounded by high, thick walls to ensure privacy. (Most walls were made of sun-dried mud bricks.) And all the servants, workers, and animals that were needed to maintain the estate lived within these walls.

The main living quarters on such an estate featured a front porch that had a roof held up by several stone columns. Beyond the porch was a corridor that led to a spacious central living room, the ceiling there also supported by columns. Usually the master bedroom was located just behind the living room. Attached to the master bedroom was a small bathroom with a tiled or stone-lined area for washing. Servants carried in water and gently poured it over the bather. According to the Greek historian Herodotus, who visited Egypt, the Egyptians were very clean. The priests, for example, "shave their bodies all over every other day," he wrote. And "they bathe in cold water twice a day and twice every night."[1]

A separate chamber or alcove off the bathroom featured a toilet. It consisted of a brick or wooden seat with

In this tomb painting, the goddess Hathor (left) wears clothes like those of wealthy Egyptian women.

a hole in the middle; below the hole was a pot that servants removed and emptied outside the walls. The walls and floors of the bathroom and other parts of the master suite were richly decorated with tiles, rugs, paintings, and other finery.

Besides these main quarters, the house had bedrooms for the master's wives, children, and other relatives. There might also be a sitting room for the family. The kitchen was a separate building resting against the inner

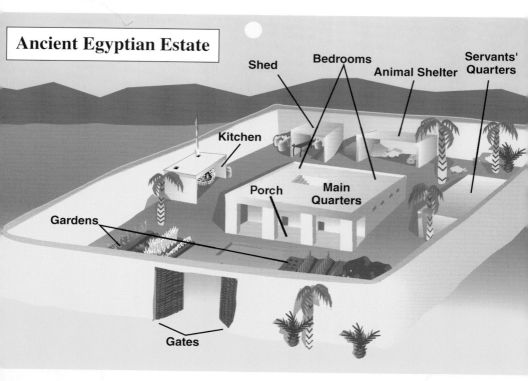

Ancient Egyptian Estate

Shed — Bedrooms — Animal Shelter — Servants' Quarters — Kitchen — Porch — Main Quarters — Gardens — Gates

side of the estate's protective wall. It featured one or more stone-lined **hearths** for cooking and tables for food preparation. Other smaller structures along the wall included servants' quarters, storage sheds, and stalls for cows, chickens, and other animals. Also inside the walls were well-kept gardens containing fruits, vegetables, and flowers.

The Pharaoh's Every Need

Of these wealthy estates, the pharaoh's was of course the biggest. In addition to his many family members and servants, hundreds of other people lived on the palace grounds. Among them were the state officials who oversaw the palace and helped the pharaoh run the country. There were also scribes, educated men who kept his records and wrote his letters. The ruler's doctors lived in-house, as did his bodyguards, maids, bakers, butchers, cooks, clothes makers, furniture makers, sculptors, chariot drivers, and many other subjects.

These people with their wide array of skills looked after the pharaoh's every need. They even groomed him and his closest family members. Each day barbers and hairdressers used razors made of bronze (a mixture of the metals copper and tin) to remove unwanted hair. The pharaoh himself was clean-shaven and wore his hair short. But by custom, he often wore wigs and false beards when appearing at court or in public. After servants had applied the ruler's wig and beard, royal dressers helped

Expert carpenters make furniture for the royal palace.

him into his court clothes. He wore a kilt with a large buckle. Much priceless jewelry, as well as sandals and a crown, completed the outfit.

Servants also applied makeup to the pharaoh's face. A green paint made from copper adorned his eyebrows and made his eyes appear slightly almond-shaped. Black paint made from lead lined his eyelids and lashes; and

At left is the outfit a pharaoh wore in battle; at right the one he wore at court.

reddish paint made from vegetable grease gave his lips extra color.

Egyptian Women

The pharaoh's queen and daughters also wore splendid clothes, jewelry, wigs, and makeup. The queen was not the ruler's only wife. Each pharaoh had a harem, a large group of wives; the queen was the head wife, with status and privileges above those of the others. The king was probably the only man in the country rich enough to keep a harem. But each of the other nobles had at least several wives.

This situation reflected the fact that, like other ancient lands, Egypt was male-dominated. In general, a woman had to do her husband's bidding. And if a man became irritated or angry with his wife, he could order her to stay in her quarters. These were usually in the rear of the house. A surviving remark by an Egyptian woman reads: "May I be sent to the back of the house if I do not speak the truth."[2] A husband could also beat his wife. But evidence shows that the law set limits on the severity of this punishment. If the woman suffered serious injury, the man could receive a hundred lashes with a whip. Or he might lose part of his property.

For the most part, though, Egyptian couples seem to have had constructive if not loving relationships. Evidence shows that upper-class husbands and wives dined, threw parties, and went hunting together. Moreover, both upper- and lower-class women shared many legal rights with men. A woman could inherit and own land, run a business, and take someone, even a man, to court.

This image of a married couple was created about 1335 B.C. His name was Meryre, hers Tener.

Indeed, Egyptian women had more freedom than their counterparts in most other ancient societies. However, only the few women born into noble and wealthy households enjoyed largely toil-free lives. This has been a benefit of the wealthy and privileged classes throughout human history.

CHAPTER TWO

Lives of the Peasant Farmers

Most ancient Egyptians were poor or nearly so. They were peasants who dwelled in small, crude houses, had no fine clothes, and could neither read nor write. The peasants endured the same desperate poverty and low social status century after century. On the one hand, most accepted their lot in life as the will of the gods. On the other, the government dealt with any protesters or rebels extremely harshly.

The vast majority of Egypt's peasants were farmers. They did not own the land they worked on. Instead, the pharaoh, temples, or nobles owned it and allowed the farmers to keep a small portion of the food grown. "A tiny share of wheat a day is all I get for my work,"[3] remarked one farmer.

The farmers' lives revolved around the mighty Nile. The world's longest river, the Nile flows south-to-north through the middle of the country and empties into the Mediterranean Sea. A narrow but moist and fertile strip of land runs along the river's banks. Outside that green ribbon stretch hundreds of miles of parched deserts; so nearly all the country's inhabitants lived near the Nile.

Farmworkers pick fruit and load it into baskets for easy transport.

All Egyptians, but especially the farmers, were dependent on the river. Each year it gently flooded over its banks and covered the fields. The water not only soaked the earth, it also laid down fresh deposits of rich soil. "When the Nile overflows," Herodotus wrote, "the whole [inhabited part of the] country is converted into a sea. And the towns, which alone remain above water, look like islands."[4] As long as these yearly floods came, Egypt produced enormous quantities of grain, more than any other Mediterranean land.

The river also provided Egyptians of all walks of life with the water they needed to drink, cook, bathe, and wash their clothes. In addition, it was a sort of liquid highway on which they sailed or rowed small boats from

Mediterranean Sea

Giza

Heliopolis

Memphis

Herakleopolis

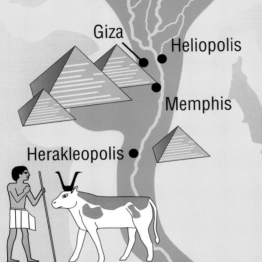

Red Sea

Valley of the Kings

Karnak

Thebes

Luxor

Hierakonopolis

The Nile River

Fertile Land

town to town. All in all, Herodotus memorably put it, Egyptian civilization was the "gift of the river."[5]

Planting and Harvesting

For Egypt's peasant farmers, the Nile's repeated rising and falling provided a way to measure time and the seasons and plan activities. They recognized three seasons. The first was *akhet,* the "inundation," when the river's waters rose and covered the land. It lasted from July through September.

Next came *peret*, which began in October when the waters retreated from the land. From then until February, farmers planted their seeds. The soil was so soft and rich that most farmers did not bother plowing first. Instead, they spread their seeds on top of the soil; then they used their plows to turn over the earth and cover them. Some farmers never plowed at all, choosing to bury the seeds by letting their sheep and pigs trample the soil. Barley, wheat, and flax (used to make clothes) were the most plentiful crops.

From February to June, the season called *shemu*, the farmers harvested these crops. Using wooden sickles, lines of reapers marched along, cutting down the wheat. Gangs of women and children followed them and gathered up the felled stalks into wicker baskets. As they toiled, they sang work songs, one of which went:

> Fair is the day dawning on the land.
> A cool breeze is rising from the north.
> The sky [remains clear], according to our wishes.
> With steady hearts, let us toil on![6]

Peasants harvest grain in this painting from the tomb of an army officer.

Later, to separate the grain from the stalks (a process called **threshing**), the farmers threw it onto a floor made of hard-beaten earth. Oxen, donkeys, or people then trampled it. Finally, workers deposited the grain into wooden or stone silos. They did this under the watchful eye of guards and overseers. These men worked for the landowners, who decided how the grain would be distributed.

Seasonal Construction Workers

No sooner had the silos filled up with grain than the Nile waters began rising again in the onset of *akhet*. During the flood season, the farmers could not work in their fields. Some busied themselves with basket-weaving and other crafts. Often, however, large numbers of peasants spent the season working on the pharaoh's building projects. This seasonal workforce of free laborers raised Egypt's massive palaces, temples, and pyramids. The workers were not slaves, therefore, as so frequently depicted in modern movies.

The largest structure built by the free peasants was the pyramid of the pharaoh Khufu, who reigned from 2589 to 2566 B.C. When Herodotus visited Egypt about two thousand years later, some Egyptian priests told him that the pyramid took twenty years to build. "It is of polished stone blocks," he wrote, "beautifully fitted, none of the blocks being less than thirty feet long."[7] Khufu's tomb required about 2.3 million of these blocks in all, each weighing an average of two and a half tons.

Not surprisingly, moving such huge stones was extremely difficult. The Egyptians did not enjoy the advan-

Peasant workers haul a heavy stone statue to the building site of a new palace.

The great pyramid of Khufu contains more than 2 million stone blocks.

tages of modern machines. Instead, they had to rely on abundant manpower, patience, and ingenuity. Teams of workers placed the stone blocks on rows of logs, which acted as rollers. To get the blocks up to the pyramid's higher levels, the workers piled up huge earthen ramps around the structure. When the work was finished, they removed the earth, revealing the finished pyramid.

A Humble Peasant Home

Almost constantly busy with field and construction work, the peasants must have spent relatively little time in their homes. At least this was true of the men. The wives, who baked, cooked, and looked after the small children, likely spent more time indoors.

The walls of a typical peasant house were made of mud bricks; the ceiling consisted of bundles of plant stems; and the floors were hard-beaten earth, sometimes covered by straw. Such a dwelling had one or two small rooms in which the occupants slept, cooked, ate, and quartered their animals. There was no bathroom, so the toilet consisted of a hole in the ground either inside or outside the house.

The Hearth

The central feature of the peasant home was the hearth, usually consisting of a flat slab of stone. Most of the poor could not afford to burn wood or charcoal. So they used dried reeds, straw, or sheep droppings for fuel. Over this fire they stewed food in earthenware pots. Such stews consisted mostly of onions, leeks, and roots. Only rarely, during religious festivals, did peasants eat meat or fruit (which the wealthy temples supplied).

The main staple of the peasant diet was bread. Bread was so important to most ancient Egyptians that they had at least fifteen different words for it. A peasant woman baked her bread in a small oven placed on or beneath her hearth. The oven was made from a large earthenware pot covered with mud. The woman pressed the bread dough into an earthenware mold and placed it in the oven. Sometimes she added butter, milk-fat, or honey to the dough to make simple pastries.

A tomb painting shows bakers mixing and kneading bread dough.

Bedtime for an average family of peasants was shortly after sundown. During the brief period of darkness before turning in, they lit their humble dwelling by burning a tiny linen wick floating in a saucer of linseed oil. Finally, they blew out the flame and retired. For Egypt's millions of poor, a good night's sleep was a welcome reward after a long day of backbreaking toil.

CHAPTER THREE

Sports and Leisure

Many surviving Egyptian wall paintings show people engaged in all manner of sports and games. Most of these pastimes were the same or similar to those popular today. They included hunting, swimming, rowing, ball-playing, wrestling, and board games, among many others.

For the most part, Egypt's farmers and other poor workers did not have much time for such leisure activities. So the more organized and formal sporting contests were the province of the well-to-do. They had plenty of leisure hours to fill as well as access to the equipment needed for activities such as hunting and rowing.

Games of the Common People

Still, the common people occasionally found time to enjoy simpler games. In particular, they looked forward to a few major religious festivals held each year. During these celebrations they were allowed to take part in various informal games. These included dancing, running, wrestling, and bouts of tug-of-war.

It is uncertain which of these games was the most popular. But a large number of painted wrestling scenes

Queen Nefertari plays *senet*, a popular board game. Each player started out with seven game pieces.

have survived, and these show clearly that Egyptian men, both rich and poor, loved to wrestle. One such group of paintings, more than four hundred in all, was found at Beni Hasan, on the Nile in central Egypt. The painted figures apply many of the same moves and holds used today in both amateur and professional wrestling. These include armlocks, headlocks, trips, shoulder throws, and numerous others.

Also, some of the paintings depict one wrestler choking another. It is unclear whether choking was considered legal or illegal. But evidence that it was probably against the rules was found in a later Egyptian sculpture. It shows some wrestlers performing for the pharaoh. One fighter applies a choke hold, and beneath are the carved words: "Take care! You are in the presence of the Pharaoh!"[8] If the pharaoh did not approve of a hold, it was probably illegal.

Outside of the religious festivals, the common people occasionally found a little time for leisure. One game played by adult men was "**water-jousting.**" Two canoes opposed each other. (These boats were small, simple craft made of bundled plant stems.) Each canoe had a few paddlers and one man standing up holding a long stick. As the paddlers moved their boats this way and that, the stickmen tried to knock each other into the water.

Meanwhile, children played a form of leapfrog. They also engaged in ball games; in one painting, two girls toss a ball back and forth while several others clap out a rhythm. In another, some children carry others piggyback; the ones riding on top are throwing a ball back and forth.

Lavish Dinner Parties

One leisure pastime the poor never enjoyed was giving and attending lavish dinner parties. Many tombs of rich Egyptians contain paintings showing banquets. The host usually greeted his guests at the main gate in the wall surrounding his estate. He then led the visitors through his gardens to the house. Once inside, the host and his most important guests sat on tall chairs, while the others sat on stools or cushions.

A stone carving depicts men water-jousting on the Nile.

The foods served at such parties included fruits, vegetables, breads, pastries, and several kinds of meat. The larger the variety and size of the spread, the more impressive and popular the host. For drinks, both wine and beer flowed freely. In one surviving painting a servant fills a woman's glass and tells her: "Drink till you are drunk! Spend the day happy!" Meanwhile, another eager guest asks, "When is the pitcher coming round to me?"[9]

Such gatherings also included entertainment. Musicians, both men and women, played harps of various sizes. They also played flutes, drums, and banjo-like stringed instruments. To this music, young women sang songs and/or performed moves similar to those of modern ballet and Broadway dancers.

In this wall painting, musicians and dancers entertain some nobles.

Hunting and Target-Shooting

The well-to-do also enjoyed athletic pursuits, especially hunting. Several descriptions of royal hunts have survived. In one, a scribe of the pharaoh Amenhotep (also known as Amenophis) III (who reigned in the fourteenth century B.C.) brags that "the total number of lions killed by His Majesty with his own arrows, from the first to the tenth year [of his reign] was 102 wild lions."[10] Another pharaoh, Thutmose III (who lived a century before Amenhotep), claimed that he bagged 120 elephants. "No king has ever done such a thing since the world began,"[11] he boasted.

These accounts are a bit misleading. Pharaohs did not generally hunt dangerous creatures such as lions and elephants in the wild. Instead, game wardens captured the animals first and then placed them in special fenced-in areas. There, carefully guarded by armed men, the pharaoh stalked and killed his prey. When hunting less dangerous animals such as antelope and wild cattle and donkeys, a ruler might venture out into the desert.

Most often the pharaoh or his nobles hunted while riding in a chariot. A driver operated the vehicle, so the hunter had both hands free to wield his weapons, either a bow and arrow or a lance. This style of hunting gave

A royal scribe hunts gazelles and other animals from his chariot.

rise to another popular sport, shooting at fixed targets from moving chariots. Sometimes the shooter tried to hit several targets in a row.

Some pharaohs went further and showed off their shooting talents in public displays. A scene carved on a stone wall shows the pharaoh Amenhotep II firing his bow from a moving chariot. Below, an **inscription** (words carved on the stone) reads: "His Majesty performed these feats before the eyes of the whole land."[12]

Again, this description is deceiving. It is almost certain that the pharaoh did not perform for poor peasants. His audience was likely limited to his nobles and soldiers. Still, Amenhotep was apparently more daring than most pharaohs. He also challenged some of his soldiers to shooting and running contests, and he gave prizes to the winners.

The Egyptians at Play

In addition, Amenhotep enjoyed one of the favorite pastimes of the ancient Egyptian nobility—rowing. A carved description of his water exploits reads:

This model boat found in a tomb shows men rowing, a popular sport among Egyptian nobles.

His arms were so strong that he was never faint when he grasped the oar and rowed his arrow-swift ship, the best of the crew of two-hundred. Many were faint after a course of half a mile, exhausted and weary of limb and out of shape; but His Majesty still rowed powerfully.[13]

The scribe no doubt exaggerated here. After all, it was customary to depict the ruler as physically, as well as, mentally superior to his subjects. Nevertheless, this account, along with many others, gives a clear picture of the Egyptians at play. Like people the world over, they recognized the need for at least an occasional break from life's more serious matters.

CHAPTER FOUR

Religion and the Afterlife

All ancient Egyptians, whether wealthy or poor, noble or peasant, were deeply religious. They were **polytheistic**, meaning that they worshiped many gods. The Egyptians carved statues to these gods, prayed to them, and **sacrificed** animals and plants to them. They also honored the gods by building temples for them.

In addition, the Egyptians devoutly believed in the existence of an afterlife. Each person hoped that when death came, his or her soul would make its way into the realm of Osiris, god of the dead. There, they believed, they would live comfortably and carefree for eternity. The privilege of reaching the afterlife did not come without cost, however. People were expected to follow various traditional, time-honored burial rituals. Those who failed to observe these rituals could not expect to enter Osiris's pleasant kingdom. For this reason, the ancient Egyptians placed a great deal of importance on burial customs.

Respect for the Gods and Life

Long before death and burial, however—indeed, all through one's life—the average Egyptian devoted much

In the tomb of King Tut, the pharaoh's mummy
rests within a large stone coffin.

time and energy to religious matters. First, it was vital to
show the gods proper respect by worshiping them on a
regular basis. People who failed to do so might not make
it into the Underworld.

The gods also expected humans to respect one another and life in general. Those who committed various
sins and crimes were likely to kindle the wrath of the
gods. And once more, the penalty was severe. Osiris himself stood at the gate of his realm and judged each person trying to enter. Some Egyptians prepared for this
judgment by memorizing the "negative confession." It

Priests and worshipers march in a procession honoring Isis, sister of Osiris, lord of the dead.

appeared in the Book of the Dead, an important collection of religious prayers and spells. The confession consisted of a series of statements, each denying that a sin had been committed. People expected to recite the confession to Osiris to win his favor. "I have not committed evil against men," one of the statements reads. Others include:

I have not blasphemed [spoken against] a god.
I have not mistreated cattle.
I have not done violence to a poor man.
I have not made anyone sick.
I have not killed anyone.
I have not taken milk from the mouths of children.[14]

Though Osiris was the final judge of the dead, the other gods had to be respected and appeased, too. The common belief was that one or more gods controlled or influenced nearly every phase of nature and daily life. Osiris did more than oversee the afterlife, for instance. He also made the Nile flood each year and inspired the growth of crops and other plants. His sister, Isis, protected children; while Thoth, usually pictured with the head of a baboon, dispensed wisdom. The goddess Hathor, who had a cow's head, oversaw dancing, music, and matters dealing with love. And the god Anubis, pictured with a jackal's head, guided people's souls to Osiris's kingdom.

The god Anubis prepares to guide a pharaoh's spirit to meet the god Osiris in the afterlife.

The Main Kinds of Worship

Public worship of these gods took place at traditional religious festivals held at certain times of the year. Priests of local temples led solemn ceremonies attended by thousands of people who journeyed from far and wide. However, families and individuals worshiped the gods more often.

The two principal kinds of worship were prayer and sacrifice. Some prayers were general chants or hymns repeated from time to time to show respect and continued devotion. "Hail to you, Ra, Lord of Truth," one such prayer began. "You who hears the prayer of him who is in captivity . . . who saves the weak from the strong."[15]

Egyptians of all walks of life also prayed for specific things. They might pray for a god to end a drought, for example. Or a person might pray to find a suitable husband or wife, or for an ill person to get well.

The other main kind of worship, sacrifice, consisted of a material gift offered to a god or gods. While in Egypt, Herodotus observed some sacrifices and later described them in his history book. Those performing a sacrifice had to follow set rituals in all stages of the ceremony, he writes. Prior to sacrificing a bull, for instance, the priest carefully examined it,

> and if he finds a single black hair on him, pronounces him unclean [not fit for the sacrifice]. He goes over him with the greatest care. . . . If the animal passes all the tests successfully, the priest marks him . . . and the penalty is death for anybody

who sacrifices an animal which has not been marked in this manner.[16]

Herodotus then lists the steps in the actual sacrifice of a bull. First, he says, the worshipers led the animal to an altar on which they had made a fire. They poured wine on the altar and called the god by name. Then they cut off the bull's head and sliced open its body. "When they have finished cutting up the bull," he continued,

> they stuff the body with loaves of bread, honey, raisins, figs . . . and other nice-smelling substances. Finally, they pour a quantity of oil over the body and burn it. . . . While the fire is consuming it, they beat their breasts.[17]

In the top half of this painting, men lead animals to sacrifice. In the lower half, they sacrifice a bull.

The common belief was that the smoke from the burning animal rose up and nourished the god. When the bull had been cooked well, the priests cut it into small portions and served these to the worshipers.

Time-Honored Burial Rituals

The Egyptians believed that performing such worship and leading an honest life would give a person a good chance of reaching the afterlife after death. Death and burial rituals were as time honored and important as those for praying and sacrificing. The first such ritual was to preserve the body. For those who could afford it, **mummification** was the best way to preserve it.

Those who transformed a corpse into a mummy were called **embalmers**. They began by removing most of the internal organs. They placed these in a special jar. (Later, mourners placed the jar beside the mummy in the tomb.)The embalmers then put the body in a vat of *natrum*, a mineral salt, for seventy days. This removed most of the body's moisture. Herodotus explained the next step, saying, "The body is washed and then wrapped from head to foot in linen cut into strips and smeared on the underside with gum."[18]

Finally, the dead person's relatives laid the mummy in a wooden or stone coffin and placed the coffin in a tomb of brick or stone. Tombs were of various shapes and sizes, depending on how well-off the family was. Not surprisingly, the pharaohs and their kin could afford the largest tombs of all. By contrast, most Egyptians could afford neither mummification nor tombs. The average family wrapped a body in a shroud of

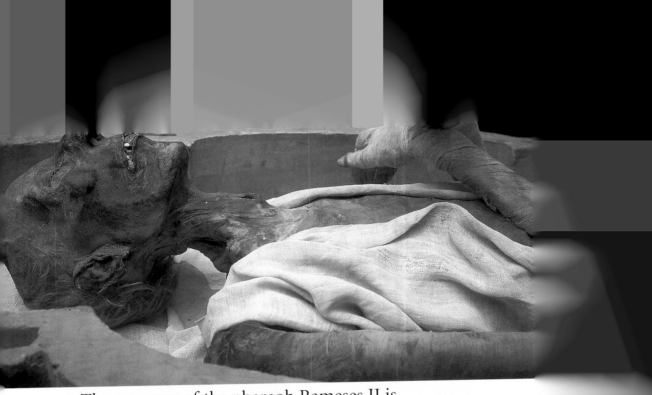

The mummy of the pharaoh Rameses II is extremely well preserved.

linen or reeds and buried it in a makeshift grave in the sand.

Both rich and poor Egyptians buried food, clothes, tools, and/or other everyday items with the body. They believed that part of the dead person's soul would need these things to sustain itself in the grave or tomb.

In the end, it mattered little whether the burial was expensive or cheap, elaborate or simple. According to Egyptian beliefs, all those who respected the gods and life and followed the accepted rituals would make it to Osiris's realm and achieve eternal life. That deeply held belief gave hope to the living and comforted families when a death occurred.

Notes

Chapter 1: Lives of the Wealthy and Privileged
1. Herodotus, *The Histories,* trans. Aubrey de Sélincourt. New York: Penguin Books, 1972, p. 143.
2. Quoted in Lionel Casson, *Daily Life in Ancient Egypt.* New York: American Heritage, 1975, p. 31.

Chapter 2: Lives of the Peasant Farmers
3. Quoted in Sergio Donadoni, ed., *The Egyptians.* Chicago: University of Chicago Press, 1997, pp. 19–20.
4. Herodotus, *Histories,* p. 165.
5. Herodotus, *Histories,* p. 131.
6. Quoted in Donadoni, *The Egyptians,* p. 11.
7. Herodotus, *Histories,* p. 79.

Chapter 3: Sports and Leisure
8. Quoted in Michael B. Poliakoff, *Combat Sports in the Ancient World.* New Haven: Yale University Press, 1987, p. 27.
9. Quoted in Casson, *Daily Life,* p. 47.
10. Quoted in Vera Olivova, *Sports and Games in the Ancient World.* New York: St. Martin's Press, 1984, p. 49.
11. Quoted in Casson, *Daily Life,* p. 49.
12. Quoted in Olivova, *Sports and Games,* p. 51.
13. Quoted in Olivova, *Sports and Games,* p. 51.

Chapter 4: Religion and the Afterlife
14. Quoted in Casson, *Daily Life,* p. 105.

15. Quoted in Richard Patrick, *All Color Book of Egyptian Mythology*. London: Octopus Books, 1972, p. 13.

16. Herodotus, *Histories*, p. 144.

17. Herodotus, *Histories*, p. 145.

18. Herodotus, *Histories*, p. 161.

Glossary

akhet: The flood season in ancient Egypt, lasting from July through September.

embalmers: People who prepare dead bodies for burial.

hearth: A fireplace or open fire used for cooking.

inscriptions: Letters and words carved into stone or other durable materials.

mummification: A process in which a human or animal body is prepared and preserved before burial.

natrum: A mineral salt used by ancient embalmers to dry out bodies and better preserve them.

peret: The planting season in ancient Egypt, lasting from October to February.

pharaoh: The ruler of ancient Egypt.

polytheistic: Worshiping multiple gods.

sacrifice: A material gift offered to a god or gods; or the act of making such a gift.

shemu: The harvest season in ancient Egypt, lasting from February to June.

threshing: The act of separating a grain from its stalks.

water-jousting: A game played by Egyptian peasants in which men in canoes tried to knock one another into the water.

For Further Exploration

Lionel Casson, *Everyday Life in Ancient Egypt.* Baltimore: Johns Hopkins University Press, 2001. A reprinted, updated version of Casson's classic *Daily Life in Ancient Egypt* (New York: American Heritage, 1975). It remains an excellent, fascinating examination of ancient Egyptian life by a great scholar.

George Hart, *Ancient Egypt.* New York: Time-Life, 1995. A very colorfully illustrated introduction to the wonders of ancient Egypt for young readers.

Anne Millard, *Mysteries of the Pyramids.* Brookfield, CT: Copper Beach Books, 1995. Aimed at basic readers, this book by a noted scholar is short but brightly illustrated and filled with interesting facts about the pyramids and ancient Egyptian life.

Neil Morris, *Atlas of Ancient Egypt.* New York: NTC Contemporary, 2000. This excellent book about ancient Egypt contains many maps and also several impressive double-page spreads on specific eras and aspects of everyday life. Highly recommended.

Don Nardo, ed., *Cleopatra.* San Diego: Greenhaven Press, 2001. The reading level of this volume is challenging for grade school students but well worth the effort. In a series of short essays, noted scholars tell nearly all that is known about this famous queen and her exploits.

Don Nardo, *Egyptian Mythology.* Berkeley Heights, NJ: Enslow, 2001. Aimed at intermediate readers, this book retells some of the most famous Egyptian myths, including the story of Osiris's murder by Seth.

Thomas Streissguth, *Life in Ancient Egypt*. San Diego: Lucent Books, 2001. A well-written introduction to ancient Egyptian life. The reading level is junior high school.

Kelly Trumble, *Cat Mummies*. Boston: Houghton Mifflin, 1999. An unusual and nicely illustrated volume that tells why cats were important in ancient Egyptian society and how these animals were mummified.

Index

Picture Credits

About the Author

A historian and award-winning writer, Don Nardo has written or edited numerous books about the ancient world. Among these are *Life in Ancient Athens, Greek and Roman Sport, Egyptian Mythology,* and Greenhaven Press's *Complete History of Ancient Greece* and *Encyclopedia of Ancient Rome.* He lives with his wife, Christine, in Massachusetts.